An Inquiry into the Religious Tenets of the Yezeedees

The Nestorians and their Rituals, Volume I.

By

George Percy Badger

First published in 1852

Published by Left of Brain Books

Copyright © 2023 Left of Brain Books

ISBN 978-1-396-32518-2

First Edition

All rights reserved. No part of this publication may be reproduced, distributed, or transmitted in any form or by any means, including photocopying, recording, or other electronic or mechanical methods, without the prior written permission of the publisher, except in the case of brief quotations permitted by copyright law. Left of Brain Books is a division of Left Of Brain Onboarding Pty Ltd.

PUBLISHER'S PREFACE

About the Book

"This is a short extract from a book by a Christian missionary which gives some historical observations on the Yezidi people of northern Iraq. For more information on the Yezidi, refer to Devil Worship: The Sacred Books and Traditions of the Yezidiz, which references this article heavily.

The Rev. Badger didn't get as close to the Yezidi as Isya Joseph did. His access was limited because he was a missionary, rather than an anthropologist. However, there aren't too many first-hand accounts of the Yezidi during the mid-nineteenth century, (actually this is the only one I've discovered so far). This document gives another perspective on this fascinating culture and their unique religious beliefs."

(Quote from sacred-texts.com)

About the Author

George Percy Badger (1815 - 1888)

"George Percy Badger (1815-1888) was a priest of the Church of England. Raised largely on Malta, he lacked formal education and credentials, but proved himself adept at languages. Badger was part of the first serious attempt of the Anglican Church to establish an Assyrian mission. He was awarded an honorary doctorate by the Archbishop of Canterbury."

(Quote from gorgiaspress.com)

CONTENTS

PUBLISHER'S PREFACE
    CHAPTER X.. 1
ENDNOTES 27

CHAPTER X.

Origin of the Yezeedees.--Yezd and Sheikh Adi designate the Supreme Being.--Yezeedee poem in honour of Sheikh Adi who is the Good Principle.--Emblems of the Deity: the sun, fire, and water, and how worshipped.--The Evil Principle.--Extract from Mrs. Badger's journal.--Sacred festivi-ties.--Sheikh Nâsir and Husein Beg.--Procession of the Melek Taoos, or the symbol of the Evil Principle.--Description of this Image.--Worship of the Evil Principle.--Magism In the religious system of the Yezeedees.--What the Yezeedees have borrowed from Christianity and Mohammedanism.--The five sacerdotal castes.--Their temporal chief.--Character of the Yezeedees.--Glimpse at their past history-They are an unpromising field for missionary exertion.

DURING our stay at Mosul in 1842-44, we made several excursions among the Yezeedees, visiting all their principal villages in the neighbourhood, and holding frequent intercourse with the beads of their community. In 1850 we resided for two months at Ba-Sheaka, where we had an opportunity of witnessing many of their religious rites and ceremonies, and of gleaning a mass of information respecting them which I shall now proceed to lay before my readers.

The family name of the tribe is Dâseni, (pl. Duasen) by which title they are frequently spoken of both by Christians and Mohammedans. They themselves also use the term, but can give no other account of its origin than that it is the ancient appellation of their race, which according to their account existed in these parts from time immemorial. Whence they sprung, from what source they derived their creed, what is meant by many of their religious observances, are subjects upon which the Yezeedees of the present day are thoroughly ignorant. In physiognomy they resemble the Coords, whose language is in general use among them, and I think it cannot be doubted that they are of the same stock with this people, and descendants of the ancient Assyrians.

The origin of the name of "Yezeedee," by which they are more commonly known, is referred by some among them to Yezeed ibn Moawiyah, but this is only a stratagem to secure their toleration by the Mohammedans. For a like purpose one of the tombs in the temple of Sheikh Adi is ascribed to Hasan-ool-Basri whereas I have been assured that the Sheikh who is said to be buried there was a different individual, and one of their own sect whose descendants are still living at Ba-Sheaka. The quotation from the Koran near the tomb was also admitted by several Kawwâls to have been introduced as a blind, and in order to prevent the Moslems from desecrating; their sacred shrine. We have already noticed a similar subterfuge as practised by the Christians of this district, and hence the convent of Mar Behnâm is commonly called "Khudhr Elias," and that of Mar Mattai "Sheikh Matta."

I think it cannot be doubted that the term "Yezeedee" is derived from Yezd, one of the titles applied by the ancient Persians to the Supreme Being. "We are Yezeedees," said Sheikh Nâsir to me on one occasion, "that is, we are worshippers of GOD." But a difficulty then arises as to the person of him whom they designate "Sheikh Adi," and who there is every reason to believe also represents the Deity in their theology. The conversation which I held with the guardians of the temple clearly leads to this conclusion, and the same has been declared to we again and again by many Yezeedees. [1] In that case his tomb must be regarded as a myth, and the prefix "Sheikh" as another artifice to throw dust into the eyes of the Mohammedan persecutors. Or it may be that "Adi" was a supposed incarnation of Yezd, who appeared on earth only for a season. This opinion receives support from the fact that several buildings are erected near his shrine to commemorate the places on which he is said to have sat.

The above hypothesis receives support from the subjoined translation of an Arabic poem, which I obtained after much trouble from the Sheikh already alluded to.

"THIS IS THE EULOGY OF SHEIK ADI; UPON HIM BE PEACE!

> "My wisdom knoweth the truth of things,
> And my truth hath mingled with me.
> My real descent is from myself;
> I have not known evil to be with me.
> All creation is under my control;
> Through me are the habitable parts and the deserts,
> And every created thing is subservient to me.
> And I am he that decreeth and causeth existence.
> I am he that spake the true word,
> And I am he that dispenseth power, and I am the ruler of the earth.
> And I am he that guideth mankind to worship my majesty,
> And they came unto me and kissed my feet.
> And I am he that pervadeth the highest heavens
> And I am he that cried in the wilderness;
> And I am the Sheikh, the one, the only one;
> And I am he that by myself revealeth things
> And I am he to whom the book of glad tidings came down
> From my Lord who cleaveth the mountains.

And I am he to whom all men came,
Obedient to me they kissed my feet.
I am the mouth, the moisture of whose spittle
Is as honey, wherewith I constitute my confidents. [2]
And by his light he hath lighted the lamp of the morning.
I guide him that seeketh my direction.
And I am he that placed Adam in my paradise.

And I am he that made Nimrod a hot burning fire.
And I am he that guided Ahmet mine elect,
I gifted him with my way and guidance.
Mine are all existences together,
They are my gift and under my direction.
And I am he that possesseth all majesty,
And beneficence and charity are from my grace.
And I am he that entereth the heart in my zeal;
And I shine through the power of my awfulness and majesty.
And I am he to whom the lion of the desert came,
I rebuked him and be became like stone.
And I am he to whom the serpent came, [3]
And by my will I made him like dust.
And I am he that shook the rock and made it tremble,
And sweet water flowed therefrom on every side.
And I am he that brought down an authentic verity,--
A book whereby I will guide the prudent ones.
And I am he that enacted a powerful law,
And its promulgation was my gift.
And I am he that brought from the fountain water
Limpid and sweeter than all waters;
And I am he that disclosed it in my mercy,
And in my might I called it the white [fountain.]
And I am he to whom the Lord of heaven said:
Thou art the ruler and governor of the universe.

And I am he who manifested some of my wonders,
And some of my virtues are seen in the things that exist.
And I am he to whom the flinty mountains bow,
They are under me, and ask to do my pleasure.
And I am he before whose majesty the wild beasts wept;
They came and worshipped and kissed my feet.
I am Adi of the mark, [4] a wanderer,
The All-Merciful has distinguished me with names.
And my seat and throne are the wide-spread earth.
In the depth of my knowledge there is no God but me.
These things are subservient to my power.
How, then, can ye deny me, O mine enemies?
Do not deny me, O men, but yield,
That in the day of the resurrection you may be happy in meeting with me.

He who dies enraptured with me, I will cast him
In the midst of paradise, after my pleasure, and by my will;
But he who dies neglectful of me
Shall be punished with my contempt and rod.
And I declare that I am the essential one:
I create and provide for thou who do my will.
Fraise he to mine essence; for all things are by my will,
And the world is lighted with some of my gifts.
I am the great and majestic king;
It is I who provide for the wants of men.
I have made known to you, O congregation, some of my ways.
Who desireth me must forsake the world.
I am he that spake a true word;
The highest heavens are for those who obey me.
I sought out truth, and became the establisher of truth;

And with a similar truth shall they attain to the highest like me.

Confused and unintelligible as much of the above rhapsody is, it tends to confirm our hypothesis that "Sheikh Adi" is one of the names of Deity in the theology of the Yezeedees. I believe this poem to be the only fragment now extant in any way connected with their creed, and I very much doubt whether they ever had any sacred Scriptures. Their occasional pretensions to possess such must he regarded as another artifice to evade the hatred of the Mohammedans, who are taught in the Korân to consider those who are not the "people of a book," i.e. have no written revelations, as fit objects for every species of indignity and persecution. Should this, however, be a mistaken conclusion, it in an indisputable fact, that hardly one Yezeedee exists who could understand a well written Arabic treatise; their Patriarch himself scarcely knows a letter of the alphabet, and his principal scribe can just read and write the colloquial dialect. So then, if they really have any books, it is clear that they can make no use of them. The notion entertained by some, that they had a secret language of their own, seems to be without foundation.

Yezd, or Sheikh Adi, is held by the Yezeedees to be the good Deity, and to him they offer their worship, which may he divided into two kinds, direct and indirect. The former consists of a few hymns, which are handed down traditionally among the Kawwâls, who may be regarded as the sacred musicians and hierophants of the sect. I have heard several of these poems repeated, but they differ little in substance from that given above, except that they are shorter, and much more unconnected. The hymns are chanted by the Kawwâls at their principal festivals to the sound of flutes and tambourines, which style of worship some among them have learned from the Christians to support by a quotation from the 150th Psalm. Their tunes are monotonous in the extreme, and the strain, though sometimes plaintive, is generally loud and harsh, and would be deemed any thing but melodious to one accustomed to the solemn harmony of our church music. Twice a year they make the pilgrimage to Sheikh Adi, where they celebrate their religious rites with great rejoicing and festivity. Mr. Layard was present on one of these occasions, and describes the uncontrollable excitement which prevailed among those present during the performance of the Kawwâls. [5] The above, so far as I have been able to learn, forms the substance of their direct worship of the Supreme Being.

The adoration of the run by the Yezeedees may be regarded as a sort of indirect homage paid to the Deity. That great luminary, as being one of the noblest productions, and most powerful agents of the divine power and goodness, is looked upon by them as the purest symbol of Yezd, and hence they worship its rising and setting by kissing the ground with their faces turned either to the east or west. This is done every morning and evening by the priestly castes; but the common people frequently omit the ceremony, and some neglect it altogether. I have been informed that the duty is only incumbent upon these latter on particular occasions, such as during the pilgrimage to Sheikh Adi, when it is performed with more than common solemnity. Large parties frequently encamp at the foot of the mountain which hems in the sacred valley on the South, and begin the ascent at early dawn. As soon as the rays of the sun touch the ground beneath them, they bow down and reverently kiss a stone, which they then place upon some other close by. We crossed this mountain on our return from the shrine, and found its surface covered with these piles, which frequently consisted of eight or ten stones raised one above the other. The same practice is observed by the heathen in India, and I have frequently seen an idol temple or pagoda surrounded with similar tokens of Pagan adoration.

Mr. Layard mentions a building and a herd of white oxen at Sheikh Adi, dedicated to "Sheikh Shems," which he supposes to be the sun. It is clear, however, that the Yezeedees so designate the place for the sake of brevity, as the entablature over the doorway records the names in full, namely, "Sheikh Shems Ali Beg and Faris," for two persons are mentioned in the inscription, which has been given entire a few pages back. In like manner the word "Shems" frequently enters into the construction of Mohammedan names.

Fire and light, as being elements cognate with that of the sun, are received by the Yezeedees as symbols of the good Deity. They never spit into a fire, and will frequently pass their hands through the flames, and make as though they would kiss and wash their faces with them, just as the Christians do with the incense in their churches. Water, also, is held by them to be a symbol of Yezd, it being a most powerful agent in communicating temporal blessings to mankind. Hence almost every fountain and spring is considered sacred, and when in their power, as those at Sheikh Adi, Ba-Sheaka, Ba-Hazâni, and others, they leave a lamp burning nightly in some adjacent niche or cave, in token of their adoration. On this account bathing is looked upon by them more in the light of a sacred duty than as an ordinary purification; and their objection to frequent the Mohammedan baths of the country has, I have no doubt, some connexion with this superstition. For the same reason they consider fish moobârak, i.e. blessed, the term which they apply to every thing sacred, and which reminds one of the aghiasmata of the Greeks. I have been informed that only a few of the lowest classes among them ever eat any produce of the waters.

The above rites and ceremonies form the sum of the religious worship offered up by the Yezeedees to the good Deity. They have no forms of prayer, and it is shocking to any Christian mind to bear them allow with the utmost indifference that they never pray. I have frequently urged upon them the duty of acknowledging their dependence on GOD on the ground of common gratitude, natural instinct, and what they admit to be due to any earthly benefactor to whom they look for help, or from whom they had received any benefits. Their only answer has been: "Such is our way; as our forefathers did before us even so do we."

I think it not improbable, however, that the reverence which they pay to their so-called Sheikhs (I mean those over whose tombs the Shaks are erected), may be regarded as another form of indirect homage rendered to the Supreme Being. I have not been able to learn who these reputed saints were, and the modern Yezeedees are quite ignorant as to the time when they lived or died. The names by which they are designated, such as Sheikh Aboo-Bekr, Sheikh Mohammed, &c., must be regarded as fictitious, and invented to conciliate the Moslems, since they do not admit the mission of their prophet or the authority of the Korân, and their Sheikhs they affirm to have lived long before Mohammed. I have often inquired whether it was not possible for a new Sheikh to rise up among them now-a-days, and the answer has been a decided negative. Sometimes they affirm that the Shaks occupy the sites where the Sheikhs have sat, sometimes where they are buried, sometimes that they are only cenotaphs, and that the bodies were interred at Sheikh Adi, and then again you are told that the Sheiks did not really die. From this I have been tempted to conclude, that these monuments may be myths, or symbols of the attributes ascribed to the Deity, or of supposed Divine emanations or incarnations. [6] Twice a year these festivals are commemorated at the different villages with the same rites as those observed at Sheikh Adi; a lamp is nightly kindled and left to burn in the Shaks called after their names, and in those to which a room is attached (as in the case of that dedicated to Sheikh Mohammed at Ba-Sheaka), the Kawwâls assemble at sunset every Tuesday and Thursday, when they burn incense over the tomb, and after watching a short time, and smoking their pipes, return home.

The season for commemorating the principal Sheikhs takes place in the month of April, and continues for eight or ten days. Ba-Sheaka and Ba-Hazâni, the adjoining village, being the two places where most of the Shaks exist, they are the great scene of Yezeedee festivities. I was absent in the Tyari country when the chief rites were performed, but Mrs. Badger having accompanied my sister and Mr. Rassam on a visit to Ba-Sheaka, took several notes of the proceedings on that occasion, which I shall insert here as illustrative of the religious customs of the Yezeedees, and as introductory to the succeeding remarks on their worship of the Evil Principle.

"April 18th, 1850.--We took a walk through the village this morning, and noticed a small enclosure which was erected by a Yezeedee last year, and who is said to have been incited thereto by the Evil Principle in a dream. The promise made to him if he obeyed was, that all persons suffering from cutaneous diseases should be cured on rubbing themselves with the dust taken from that spot. After visiting the fountain, where we saw a number of females performing their ablutions in preparation for the coming feast, we went to the shrine of Sheikh Mohammed, situated in a pretty grove of olive-trees. Part of the court of this building serves as a kitchen, in which were a number of Yezeedees engaged in slaughtering ten sheep destined to be eaten this evening by the community. There was also a large stock of food in the place, which had been furnished by the villagers, each according to his ability, to be distributed among the poor. We next entered the shrine through a low entrance, and found there a broken cabinet inlaid with mother-of-pearl, which is said to cover the remains of the Sheikh. The enclosure round the shrine contains several other tombs, and a number of small apartments.

"This being new year's day with the Yezeedees we again walked through the villages to witness their festivities, and observed a number of wild scarlet anemonies stuck over the entrance to several of the houses. We learned on inquiry that these were intended to propitiate the Evil Principle, and to ward off calamity during the coming year. The practice reminded me at once of the blood sprinkled upon the door-posts of the dwellings of the Israelites in Egypt as a sign for the destroying angel to pass over, and it also recalled to my memory a custom prevalent among the Hindoos and Parsees of India, who hang a string of leaves across the entrance to their houses at the beginning of every new year.

"On our return home we had a visit from five Kawwâls who brought with them their flutes and tambourines, and entertained us with what they styled their sacred music. During the performance they put themselves into all kinds of unnatural contortions, swinging their bodies to and fro, and uttering strains which were anything but solemn or harmonious. Mr. Rassam requested them to play some more cheerful airs, but this they declined on the ground that the day was consecrated to religious observances.

"In the evening we again visited the shrine to see the Yezeedees partake of the feast which had been prepared for them during the day; but being rather late we met the guests as they were leaving the place, some with their mouths full, others wiping them with their sleeves, and looking as if they had enjoyed themselves exceedingly. We were then invited by those who acted as waiters on the occasion to partake of the entertainment. A carpet was accordingly spread before the shrine for our accommodation, and dishes of mutton cut up into small pieces, wheat boiled in sour milk, and six new wooden spoons were laid before us. I was struck with the cleanliness of the food and the vessels in which it was served, as also with the general neatness of the people. After we had tasted of the different dishes, the place was again swept, an old Yezeedee near observing the meanwhile that 'cleanliness is next to heaven.' A number of Kawwâls sat smoking in the court-yard waiting the coming of Sheikh Nâsir, their religious head, who had just reached the village and was expected to conduct their sacred ceremonies the same night. We made many inquiries respecting the object of these festivities, but the Yezeedees were by no means communicative: all they informed us was that on the present occasion they celebrated the nuptials of Sheikh Mohammed, whom they believe to be married once every year.

"On reaching home we received a visit from Sheikh Nâsir, who wits accompanied by a younger brother of Husein Beg, the temporal Yezeedee chief, by several Kawwâls, and a large retinue of servants. He appeared a very quiet humble man, with a benevolent but sorrowful countenance. He spoke feelingly of the indignities to which those Yezeedees were subjected who were forced into the army, and complained that they were not only ill-treated and persecuted by the Turkish soldiers, but were made to put on uniform of a colour which it was unlawful for any of their community to wear, and moreover to eat prohibited food, and to frequent the bath, which for them was a sin. I understood afterwards that the colour objected to was blue, especially dark blue; [7] and that the prohibited vegetables were lettuce and cabbage. A new levy of soldiers was about to take place, which seemed to cast a gloom over Sheikh Nâsir and the Yezeedees generally.

"On leaving the chief told us that he should spend the night with the Kawwâls in the shrine of Sheikh Mohammed, where the principal religious ceremonies were to be performed. What those were we could not learn, but were told that they danced to the music of the tambourines and flutes. This evening none of the cattle were milked, but all the cows, sheep, and goats with their young were turned out into the fields, and permitted to feast themselves at their pleasure.

"April 19th.--This morning the sound of fife and drum at dawn of day announced that the recreative part of the festival had commenced; so after an early breakfast we repaired to the vicinity of the shrine near which a large concourse of Yezeedees Lad already assembled, all habited in their best holiday suits. The men were clad in clean and gaudy-coloured jackets and turbans, the women in silk and satin garments, their necks hung round with ornaments, and their head-dresses covered with rows of silver coin. All carried in their turbans a bouquet of flowers, among which the rose and anemone were the most conspicuous, interspersed with an occasional ostrich feather dyed scarlet. About two hundred now joined hand in hand and formed themselves into a ring round a couple of musicians who played on a drum and kind of lute. The merry strain was at first slow, but quickened as it proceeded, the dancers the meanwhile keeping time with their arms which were thrown violently backwards and forwards as they moved round and round again, alternately narrowing and widening the circle by advancing and retreating two long and two abort steps. The varieties of form and feature, the animated countenances, the rich dresses, long flowing sleeves waving to and fro and seeming to keep time with the measured paces of the performers, made up a lively scene, and reminded me of the merry-making at an English fair. No little coquetry was displayed by the younger girls both in dress and manners, and several were pointed out to me as being joined hand in hand with their future husbands. At a short distance from this group were a number of gaily dressed

Yezeedees mounted on horse-back, amusing themselves with the more manly sport of throwing the jereed, and in running races. They soon got tired of this, however, and politely joined the ladies, into whose faces they peered with something very much akin to impudence. Many of them had evidently a particular object in view, and the musicians abetted them in the search by playing a very slow tune, so as to allow them a better opportunity of examining each damsel as she moved round in the dance. I was afterwards informed that these rencontres generally lead to matrimonial engagements.

"After returning home we received a visit from Husein Beg, the temporal head of the Yezeedees, who had come hither to join in the festivities. From what passed on this occasion we learned that much jealousy existed between him and Sheikh Nâsir, on account of the greater influence which the latter seems to possess among the Yezeedees. Husein Beg is but a stripling, and has three wives already; his father, it is said, had a new wife every week.

"Having heard that the Melek Taoos [literally King Peacock] was to be exhibited in the village, we made every effort to learn all particulars respecting it, and were informed by Sheikh Nâsir, who, together with Husein Beg and many of the principal Yezeedees dined with us this evening, that it would be brought in procession from Ba-Hazâni to Ba-Sheaka on the following day. Accordingly we sallied forth hoping to get a sight of this mysterious idol. On arriving at the outskirts of the village, we heard the sound of music, and hastening to the spot from whence it came, saw the procession slowly advancing, but no sooner did they catch a glimpse of our party than they hid the Senjak. [8] The harsh and deafening noise of the pipes and tambourines still went on, however, and we stood silent spectators of the scene. Two Peers preceded the bearer of the sacred cock, carrying burning censers in their hands which they waved to and fro, filling the air with the odour of the incense. As they passed along the bystanders bowed themselves in adoration, uttering some indistinct sentences the meanwhile, and immersed their hands in the smoke with which they perfumed their arms and faces. The Senjak was then carried to the house of the old Kiahya, or head, of the village (he having been the highest bidder for the honour of entertaining it on this occasion,) where it remained for two days, during which time all profane festivities were suspended.

"Being still anxious to penetrate into the mystery of this sacred symbol, we solicited Sheikh Nâsir to allow us to see it, which, after much ado, he finally promised, and fixed the next morning for our visit, when most of the villagers would be absent on a religious excursion to Ain-oos-Safrâ. His consent, however, was given, on condition that my sister-in-law and I should go to the house unattended. At the time appointed, a respectable Yezeedee came to conduct us to the place, which to our astonishment we found thronged with people. We were then ushered into an open recess where about thirty Kawwâls and Peers were seated in two rows. On entering, the whole party rose, and after the usual eastern salutation, coffee was served: but Sheikh Nâsir was not forthcoming, neither could we see any traces of the Cock. On inquiring whether they had not received directions to show us the Senjak, they replied in the negative, and further assured us that it could not be exhibited to us unless Sheikh Nâsir or Husein Beg were present. We were not a little annoyed at this disappointment. Mrs. Rassam and I having had to brook the vulgar gaze of so many men; but resolving not to be discouraged, we again sent to Sheikh Nâsir, calling upon him to fulfil his promise. The messenger noon returned to tell us that all was now ready, but that we must still go unaccompanied by any other person. We found the house more crowded than before, and were again conducted to the recess, where

Husein Beg, two Peers, and a few Sheikhs were seated. At the end of the apartment on a raised platform, was the famous Senjak, which we were permitted to examine as near as we chose. The figure is that of a bird, more resembling a cock than any other fowl, with a swelling breast, diminutive head, and wide spreading tail. The body is full, but the tale flat and fluted, and under the throat is a small protuberance intended perhaps to represent a wattle. This is fixed on the top of a candlestick, round which are two lamps, placed one above the other, and each containing seven burners, the upper being somewhat larger than the under. The whole is of brass, and so constructed, that it may be taken to pieces and put together with the greatest case. Close by the stand was a copper jug, filled with water, which we understood was dealt out to be drunk as a charm by the sick and afflicted. A Fakîr was in the room relating all the benefits that had been conferred on Christians and Mohammedans, as well as on Yezeedees, by the contributions to the Senjak, and calling upon all present to give liberally to the same object. The following is a sketch of the famous symbol which I committed to paper on my return home."

THE MELEK TAOOS OF THE YEZEEDEES

According to the theology of the Yezeedees, Melek Taoos, of which the Senjak is a type, is the principle or power from whom all evil proceeds, and their religious Services seem to partake much more of a propitiatory than of an eucharistic character. In this respect, their system is in accordance with the natural feelings of man in his fallen state, which lead him rather to dread punishment for his misdeeds, than to be thankful for benefits received. The Yezeedees, therefore, revere the evil principle, not out of love, but from fear, and this reverence they manifest not only by such religious rites as these already described, but by scrupulously avoiding all mention of Satan, and the use of any word implying execration. Thus, they will never pronounce the word "Sheitan," the Arabic for Devil, nor "Shat," a river, because of its resemblance to the former. Neither will they use any part of the verb "laan," to curse, nor "naal, naalbend," a horse-shoe, a farrier, because the two latter have nearly the same sound, and all express the much dreaded attribute of Melek Taoos. Their use of the scarlet anemone as a propitiatory charm or offering, has already been mentioned, and if this flower is chosen for its colour, we may see in it, as well as in the ochre with which the heathen in India daub their idols, a symbol of blood and sacrifice.

What the particular rites are wherewith the Yezeedees testify their veneration for the evil principle in their secret assemblies, I am unable to state from personal observation; but I received the following account from one who has frequently been an eyewitness of them. It appears, there are in all seven [9] brazen cocks, which are constantly being carried about in some or other of the Yezeedee districts. These are under the absolute control of Sheikh Nâsir, who directs their line of march, and in what places they are to be exhibited. The honour of entertaining the sacred symbol is accorded to the highest bidder, and I have heard that Sheikh Nâsir is entitled to a tithe of the contributions collected on these occasions. The successful competitor having made all the necessary preparations, the cock is set up at the end of a room, and covered with a white cloth, underneath which is a plate to receive the subscriptions. At a given signal all rise up, each approaches the Senjak, bows before it, and throws his contribution into the plate. On returning to his place, each worships the image several times, and strikes his breast, as if to propitiate the favour of the much dreaded principle.

It will appear from the above, that the worship of Melek Taoos is much more common among the Yezeedees than that of Sheikh Adi. I have frequently inquired the cause of this, and the answer has been, that the latter is so good that he needs not to be invoked, whereas the former is so bad, that he requires to be constantly propitiated. As these two principles seem to form the substance of their religious creed, there can be no doubt as to its origin. "The great and fundamental article of the Persian theology," writes Gibbon, "was the celebrated doctrine of the Two Principles; a bold and injudicious attempt of Eastern philosophy to reconcile the existence of moral and physical evil, with the attributes of a beneficent Creator and governor of the world." Such was pure Zoroastrianism, which in after ages was corrupted by the Persian Magians by a various mixture of foreign idolatry. This was borrowed chiefly from the Sabeans, whose religion had been diffused over Asia, by the science of the Chaldeans, and the arms of the Assyrians. Of this people, the author above quoted says: "The flexible genius of their faith was always ready, either to teach or to learn; in the tradition of the creation, the deluge and the patriarchs, they held a singular agreement with their Jewish captives; they appealed to the secret books of Adam, Seth, and Enoch; and a slight infusion of the Gospel has transformed the last remnant of the Polytheists, into the Christians of S. John, in the territory of Bassora." It is not within the scope of this work to trace with precision, the relation existing between the modern Yezeedees and the Magians of old; enough has been advanced to show that the religious system of both took its rise from the famous prophet and philosopher of the Persians, and the after history of the Yezeedees, their admixture with Christians, and subjection to Moslem rule, will fully account for any variations in their present opinions and rites, from those which they originally professed and practised. [10]

I am of opinion, however, that the modern Yezeedees have borrowed little from Christianity beyond what was incorporated into their system by their more learned and zealous forefathers, when the Gospel was first proclaimed in these parts. Their professed reverence for our blessed LORD seems to arise more from the difficulty of withholding from Him the honour which is universally ascribed to His character and dignity, than from any knowledge which they possess of His person or mission. In this respect, indeed, they are profoundly ignorant, and their confession of Isa, the Son of Mary, is much more undefined and imperfect than that of the Mohammedans. It is true that they affect more attachment to Christians than to Mussulmans; but this may be fully accounted for on other ground than that of any sincere respect for Christianity. For ages the Christians have been co-sufferers with them, they have lived under the same yoke of bondage and oppression, and this community of endurance has doubtless tended to engender something akin to sympathy between the two parties.

Beyond this vague acknowledgment of the SAVIOUR of mankind, and an equally uncertain homage which they profess to render to the prophets arid apostles, as well as to the Old [11] and New Testament Scriptures, the Yezeedees practise no rites distinctively Christian. Their ceremonial washings at Sheikh Adi, which have been thought by some to be borrowed from the Sacrament of Holy Baptism, have a much closer resemblance to an almost universal practice among the heathen, who deem it an act of devotion to bathe in the pools near which their temples are erected. And not only are these ablutions repeated at every new visit to the shrine of Sheikh Adi, but many other streams and ponds are held sacred by the Yezeedees, and are frequented by them on particular occasions for the same purpose.

Mr. Layard is mistaken when he states that the "Yezeedee year begins with that of the eastern Christians." It began this year (1850) on the 17th of April, and the inscriptions on all their monuments are dated from the Hegira. The festival of the new year must always be kept on Wednesday, which with Friday, they seem to consider the most sacred days in the week. The service already described as being performed at the Shaks of Sheikh Mohammed every Tuesday and Thursday after sunset has respect to these two days,--as the day with all easterns begins at that time. Friday, however, may be observed to conciliate the Mohammedans. None fast on these days, nor do any abstain from work; in fact the visit of a few Kawwâls to the village shrines seems to be the only rite by which these days are hallowed. The only fast of the Yezeedees is kept for three successive days in the month of December, when they profess to commemorate the death of Yezeed ibn Moawiyah. This also I consider another artifice to conciliate the bigotry and intolerance of their Mohammedan rulers. Their seeming neglect of this exercise may be regarded as another feature of Magism, since Zoroaster, as is well known, condemned fasting as a criminal rejection of the best gifts of Providence.

Sufficient has already been said by way of accounting for the different traces of Mohammedanism which are to be met with in the creed and practices of the modern Yezeedees. My conviction is that they have no real respect for any of the distinctive doctrines of Islâm, and if a few of their Fakîrs have learned to read a chapter or two of the Koran, the unwelcome task has been undertaken with the same object, viz. in order that their sect may be the more readily tolerated, or for the sake of learning the language of their rulers. Circumcision cannot be regarded as a distinctive Mohammedan rite, nor is it deemed indispensable by the Yezeedees. The large tribe of the Khaletiyeh on the Tigris about Radhwân do not practise circumcision, nevertheless they are held to be orthodox Yezeedees.

The sacerdotal order of the Yezeedees, like that of the Magi of old, is extremely numerous, and it; divided into five castes which are prohibited from intermarrying, and are thus kept distinct. The first in dignity is Sheikh Nâsir, who may be regarded as the patriarch or supreme Pontiff of the whole sect. This office is hereditary in the family, and generally descends to the first-born son. It is the province of the of the Great Sheikh to direct all the religious affairs of the community, to lead in their sacred rites at certain times, and to send teachers to the different districts. The present incumbent possesses considerable property, and engages in extensive agricultural pursuits. Twice a year he visits most of the villages in the neighbourhood to collect contributions in the shape of free-will offerings, and he commissions deputies to the more distant provinces for the same purpose. The Yezeedees believe him to be endued with supernatural powers, and his mediation is often sought to heal obstinate diseases in men and cattle, to make the barren fruitful, to crown a journey or other undertaking with success, &c. which he affects to do by charms and other occult means. Mohammed, Mr. Rassam's Kawass, or orderly, who is a strict and sincere Mussulman, and cordially hates all unbelievers, especially such as possess no books, assured me that his wife Miriam, originally a Yezeedee, was cured of epilepsy by Sheikh Nâsir. He had tried the native physicians, the piety of the Moollahs, and afterwards the skill of an able Frank surgeon, who treated her for several months; but all to no purpose. At length, in spite of all his prejudices, he took her to the great Yezeedee Sheikh, who, he informed me, first directed him to slaughter a sheep, with the blood of which he sprinkled her forehead, then covered her breast with a coating of bitter clay brought from Sheikh Adi, tied a string over her left wrist, and kept her in a separate room for seven days, feeding her upon a particular kind of bread which he prepares with his own hands. Several years have now elapsed, and Mohammed declares that his wife has never had a single attack since she left the roof of Sheikh Nâsir. Knowing his antipathy for the Yezeedees, I asked him how he accounted for the possession of such power by an unbeliever. "It puzzled me very much," said he, "but on applying to Moollah Sultan for a solution of the difficulty, he told me that it was natural that the unclean should cast out the unclean!"

Sheikh Nâsir sometimes takes part in celebrating the marriages of persons of distinction among his community. The contract is generally settled by the relations of the two parties, but the bond is scaled by the bridegroom going to the Great Sheikh, and receiving from him a loaf of consecrated bread, half of which is eaten by himself and the other half by his bride.

The Peers and Kawwâls are empowered to exercise the same functions, for which they receive a fee. Sheikh Nâsir is also occasionally solicited to preside over the funeral rites, which are more generally conducted by the Kawwâls and Sheikhs. These are extremely simple, but in one respect peculiar: when a Yezeedee is about to die, a Kawwâl is called in, who pours into his mouth a quantity of water; if he happens to die before this ceremony can he performed it is reserved till the body is brought to the grave. [12] Whilst the corpse is laid out in the house, the Kawwâls chant one or two hymns to the sound of their sacred instruments, and then precede the funeral procession to the grave, burning incense as they go. Morning and evening for several successive days the male and female relatives of the deceased repair to the grave in distinct parties, the women to weep and mourn, and the men to burn incense, and watch a short time in silence round the spot. It strikes me that these rites go to support the hypothesis already advanced, and that as a symbol of Yezd or Sheikh Adi, the life-giving principle, the infusion of water is intended to typify, or is supposed to convey, vitality after death. Some would fain deny it for fear of reproach, but I think there can be no doubt that the Yezeedees hold the doctrine of the metempsychosis.

The next in dignity are the PEERS, or Elders, who are few in number compared with the other minor orders of the priesthood. In a Subordinate degree they are Supposed to possess the powers, and permitted to exercise the functions of the Pontiff, and frequently act as his deputies.

The SHEIKHS may be regarded as the scribes of the Sect, though few of them can write. Sheikh Nâsir, who has already been mentioned as having furnished me with the eulogy of Sheikh Adi, belongs to this order, and is perhaps one of the most learned among them. He can spell over a few chapters of the Koran, and write a tolerable hand; but he could not explain to me the meaning of several words in the Yezeedee poem.

The Kawwâls [13] have been so frequently brought before the reader in the exercise of their peculiar office, that little further needs to be added under this head. They are the musicians of the community, and as music and dancing form so important a part in the worship of the Yezeedees, theirs is the most numerous of all the sacerdotal castes. They are confined to the villages of Ba-Sheaka and Ba-Hazâni, but are frequently sent to other parts to conduct the religious services of the people, for which they receive remuneration.

The Fakîrs are the lowest order in the Yezeedee hierarchy; it is their province to minister at Sheikh Adi, as hewers of wood and drawers of water, and to attend the Cock in its peregrinations. They carry a band on their left shoulder with which they tie up the faggots for the shrine, and are sometimes called Kara-bash, or Black-heads, from always wearing a turban of that colour. They are also employed in collecting contributions for the temple, and in this respect they resemble the begging friars of monastic establishments.

Besides the above, the Yezeedees have a temporal chief, which dignity is also hereditary and confined to one family. Husein, the present Emeer, exercises a kind of conventional authority over the entire sect, and is the medium through which the local government communicates to them its wishes and orders. He exercises great influence among them, and, what appears rather strange, possesses the prerogative of cutting off any refractory member from the privileges of the community. From all I have heard, this punishment imposes far greater penalties upon the offenders than the severest form of excommunication as practised by Christians, and is much dreaded by the Yezeedees.

I shall now add a few words on the general character of this people. The Yezeedees, particularly those in the district about Mosul, are a very industrious race, clean in their habits, and quiet and orderly in their general behaviour. Many of them, however, are very intemperate in the use of arrack, and some make a boast before Christians of the superiority of their religion to that of Islâm, inasmuch as it does not prohibit the use of intoxicating liquors. Drunken broils, however, such as are, alas! too common in our own land, are almost unknown among them, and the native Christians with whom they dwell, bear witness that in their general intercourse with other sects, they are comparatively free from many of those known immoralities which pollute the lives and conduct of Mohammedans; though it in said that great lewdness secretly prevails within the limits of their own community. This is a natural result of polygamy, which is allowed among them to the extent of three wives, to the facility of obtaining divorce, and particularly to the frequency of incestuous marriages. Instead of being deemed a crime, it is generally thought desirable and praiseworthy, for a man to marry his sister-in-law, and for a woman to marry her brother-in-law.

During the government of the different hereditary pashas of these districts, and when anarchy frequently prevailed throughout the country, the Yezeedees occasionally got the upper hand, and the people of Mosul still remember the time when Christians and even Mohammedans did not dare to enter the mountain-pass in which Sheikh Adi is situated, for fear of being robbed or murdered. The Yezeedees of Sinjâr were the terror of all caravans and merchants travelling through the desert, few of whom escaped without being attacked and plundered. In 1832 the Coordish pasha of Rawandooz, instigated thereto by religious fanaticism and a thirst for booty, fell upon those inhabiting the plains, burned their villages, carried many of them away captive, and on the mound of Kayoonjuk massacred several thousands in cold blood who had fled thither, hoping that the people of Mosul would offer them a refuge within the city walls. About six years later Mohammed Pasha led an army against the Yezeedees of Sinjâr, and after several defeats finally succeeded in crushing their power, and in reducing them to abject submission by the most cruel and barbarous measures. And as late as 1814, when Jebel Toor was under the government of Bedr Khan Beg, the Yezeedees of that district were subjected to the most wanton oppression by that tyrannical Coord, in order to force them to embrace Islamism. Many underwent imprisonment, stripes, and other indignities, and a few angered death, rather than renounce their creed; but seven entire villages became the professed followers of the False Prophet.

The Tanzeemât Khairiyyeh, or Beneficial Ordinance, lately issued by the Sultan, has wrought a great change in the local administration of the Turkish provinces, and the Yezeedees are now free from many of those exactions and hardships under which they formerly laboured. An imperial edict has also been issued permitting such as were made Mohammedans by force to return to their own creed; and the Yezeedees in Jebel Toor are just beginning to recover from the effects of their former servitude and oppression.

ENDNOTES

[1] May not the Yezeedee "Adi" be cognate with the Hebrew אד Adh or Ad, the two first letters in the original of Adonai, the Lord, and its compounds Adonijah, Adonibezek, &c.? This derivation is open to objection on the ground that the Yezeedees write the word with ע and not with א. Little weight, however, ought to be attached to this fact, since they write it so only in Arabic, of which they know but very little, and not in their own language which they do not write at all. Moreover they may have assimilated the mode of expressing the title of their Deity in by-gone days to that of Adi, one of the descendants of the Merawiyan caliphs, with whom from fear of being persecuted by the Mohammedans, they sometimes identify him. It is supposed by some that the "Sheikh Adi" of the Yezeedees, is the same with "Adi," one of the disciples of Mani; but this, I think, improbable, since there is no proof that even Mani himself was deified by his followers. (p. 2)

[2] Derwishes among the Mohammedans are inducted into office by drinking a bowl of milk into which a Sheikh has spat, which ceremony is called Hâl by the Arabs. The original word which I have translated "Confidents," designates literally those learned men whom eastern monarchs used to entertain at their courts. The term as above applied seems to indicate the Kawwâls who are the sacred poets of the Yezeedees. (p. 4)

[3] The façade of the temple at Sheikh Adi bears the figure of a lion and serpent, as may be seen from the sketch already referred to. (p. 4)

[4] The original word is Esh-Shâmi, which the ignorant Yezeedees think to mean "the Damascene," and hence they frequently say that Sheikh Adi came from Damascus. The spirit of the passage has guided me in the rendering above given, which is supported by the context. (p. 5)

[5] Nineveh and its Remains, Vol. I. p. 293. (p. 7)

[6] It in a well known fact, that many of these monuments have been raised within the last century. The four walls are first built, some time after these are roofed in, and eventually the cone is superadded. I have no doubt that the enclosure, to be mentioned presently, will ere long be converted into a Shaks. (p. 9)

[7] This prejudice against blue seems to spring from reverence for that colour. There is a dyeing establishment at Ba-Hazâni kept by Christians, where indigo is the only dye used. This place is considered sacred by the Yezeedees; who frequently resort thither to kiss the door-posts. (p. 12)

[8] Senjak is the name by which the Yezeedees generally designate this sacred image. The word means literally a Banner. (p.14)

[9] This seems to be a sacred number with the Yezeedees. The reader will remember, that the two lamps on the Senjak, already described, had each seven burners. We are reminded here of the worship of the Sabeans, of whom Gibbon thus writes: "They adored the seven gods, or angels, who directed the course of the seven planets, and shed their irresistible influence on the earth. The attributes of the seven planets, with the twelve signs of the zodiac, and the twenty-four constellations of the northern and southern hemispheres, were represented by images and talismans; the seven days of the

week were dedicated to their respective deities." It in worthy of note, moreover, that the sceptre engraved on the front of the temple of Sheikh Adi has seven branches. (p. 17)

[10] Mr. Layard, in his "Nineveh and its Remains," (Vol. II. p. 462) gives the annexed sketch of a bird from one of the slabs dug up at Nimrood:

to which he subjoins the following note. "The Iynges, or sacred birds, belonged to the Babylonian and probably to the Assyrian religion. They were a kind of demons, who exercised a peculiar influence over mankind, resembling the ferouher of the Zoroastrian system. The oracles attributed to Zoroaster describe them as powers animated by GOD.

> Νοούμεναι Ἴυγγες παρόθεν νοέουσι καὶ αὐταί.
> Βουλαῖς ἀφθέγκτοις κινούμεναι ὥστε νοῆσαι.'

(Zoroaster, Oracul. Magn. ad Calcem Oracul. Sybill. ed. Gall. p. 80; and Cary's Fragments, p. 250.) Their images made of gold were in the palace of the King of Babylon, according to Philostratus. (Lib. i. c. 25, and lib. vi. c. 2.) They were connected with magic. (Selden, de Diis Syriis, p. 39.) It is possible that the bird borne by warriors, in a bas-relief from the centre palace. way represent the Iynges."

There can be little doubt, but that the Melek Taoos is in substance the ferouher of Zoroastrianism; and I think it very probable, that this Image in used for purposes of divination in the secret assemblies of the modern Yezeedees. The worship of a bird appears to have been a most ancient species of idolatry; it in condemned expressly in Dent. iv. 16, 17: "Lest ye corrupt yourselves and make you a graven image, the similitude of any figure the likeness Of any fowl that flieth in the air." (p. 19)

[11] The cosmogony of the Yezeedees is different from that of the Old Testament Scriptures. They sometimes speak as though they agreed with us on this subject; but I am persuaded that they believe the world to have existed long before Adam. From several remarks which dropped from their Sheikhs, I am inclined to think that they hold the eternity of matter. (p. 19)

[12] The reader will here remember a practice common among the Brahmins of India, who pour water from the Ganges into the mouth of the dying. (p. 22)

[13] Kawwâl literally means one who can speak fluently, an orator.

It has been my lot to know much of this people under their adverse as well as under their more prosperous circumstances, and my conviction is that they present the most unpromising field I know of for missionary exertion. They are ignorant to a proverb, and entertain the strongest prejudices against learning of every kind. They are neither communicative nor frank when inquired of respecting their own religious system, and manifest the greatest indifference whenever any attempt is made to expound to them the doctrines of Christianity. With God all things are possible; but humanly speaking there seems little hope of the conversion of these heathen until the native churches shall have risen from sleep, and again trimmed their lamps with a zeal and love such as were exhibited in the early Nestorian missionaries, who earned the glad tidings of the Gospel into the wilds of Tartary, and planted the banner of the cross among the refined pagans of China. (p. 23)

www.ingramcontent.com/pod-product-compliance
Lightning Source LLC
Chambersburg PA
CBHW051554010526
44118CB00022B/2709